WOLF SPIDERS

Blaine Wiseman

SPIDERS

AV2
www.av2books.com

Step 1
Go to **www.av2books.com**

Step 2
Enter this unique code
DMBWOPEDV

Step 3
Explore your interactive eBook!

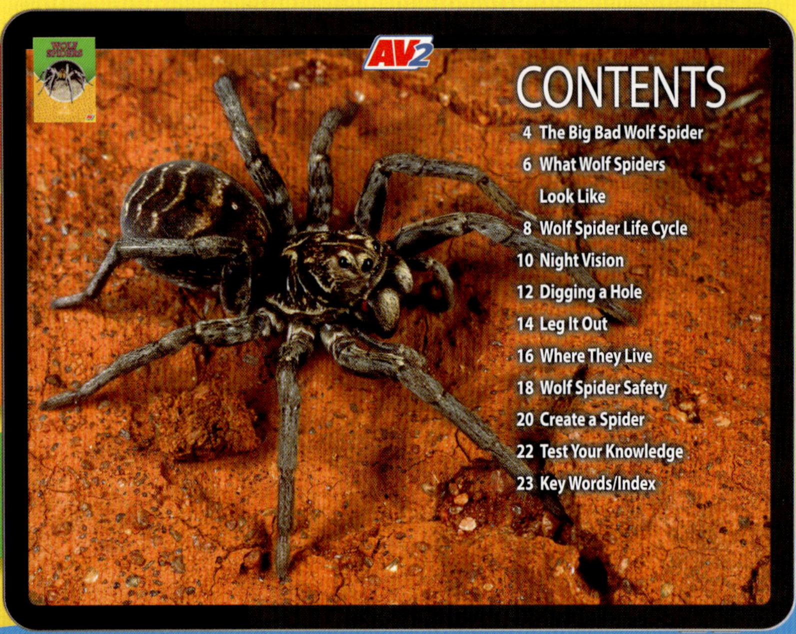

AV2 is optimized for use on any device

Your interactive eBook comes with...

Contents
Browse a live contents page to easily navigate through resources

Audio
Listen to sections of the book read aloud

Videos
Watch informative video clips

Weblinks
Gain additional information for research

Try This!
Complete activities and hands-on experiments

Key Words
Study vocabulary, and complete a matching word activity

Quizzes
Test your knowledge

Slideshows
View images and captions

... and much, much more!

SPIDERS

WOLF SPIDERS

Contents

Introduction

The Big Bad Wolf Spider

Wolf spiders are excellent hunters. They are known as fast runners. Wolf spiders get their name because they hunt like wolves. Wolf spiders do not use webs. Instead, they chase after and pounce on their **prey**. They grab it with their legs and **pedipalps**.

Wolf spiders use their pedipalps to hold on to food as they eat.

Parts of a Spider

What Wolf Spiders Look Like

Wolf spiders are covered in hairs. These spiders are dark in color. This helps them stay **camouflaged**.

The easiest way to know if a spider is a wolf spider is by its eyes. Wolf spiders have eight eyes in three rows. The bottom row has four small eyes. The middle row has two large eyes. The top row has two large eyes near the sides of the head.

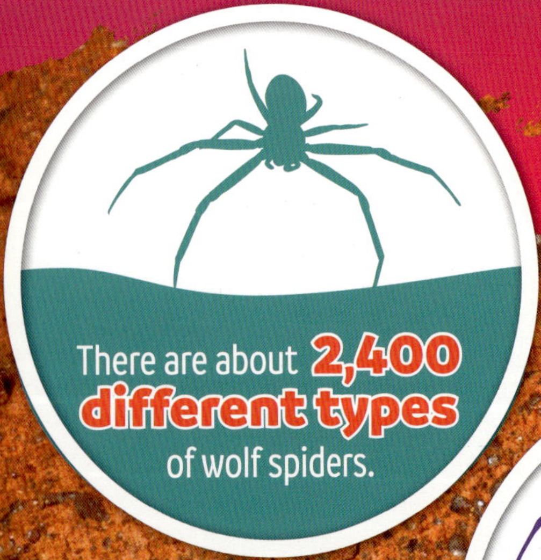

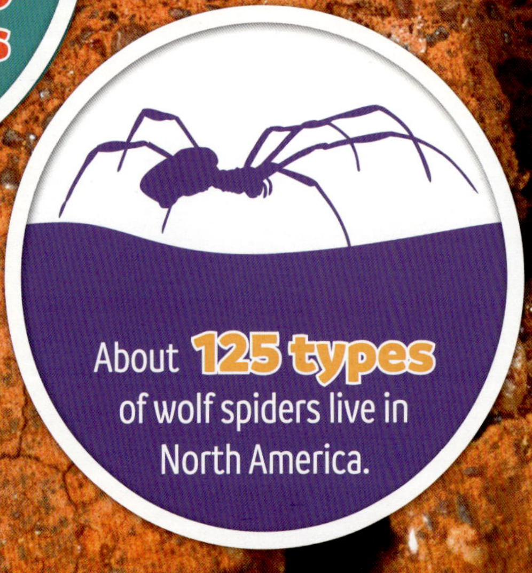

Wolf Spider Life Cycle

Female wolf spiders dig **burrows** or build nests. Males wander to find a **mate**. They attract females by making spider music. They drum their pedipalps to make a noise.

A wolf spider lays more than a hundred eggs. She carries them in a silk egg sac. Once the eggs hatch, the wolf **spiderlings** climb on their mother's back. After a few weeks, they can live on their own. Female wolf spiders live for several years. Males usually live for one year or less.

Sizing It Up

Zebra Jumping Spider
Leg Span: 0.3 inches (0.8 centimeters)

Western Black Widow Spider
Leg Span: 1.5 inches (3.8 cm)

Carolina Wolf Spider
Leg Span: 3 inches (7.6 cm)

Giant Golden Orb Weaver
Leg Span: 5.9 inches (15 cm)

Giant Huntsman Spider
Leg Span: 12 inches (30.5 cm)

Goliath Birdeater
Leg Span: 12 inches (30.5 cm)

Night Vision

Wolf spiders have excellent eyesight. They see better than most other kinds of spiders. Their eyes help them hunt.

Wolf spider eyes **reflect** light. This lets them see better at night. They can sneak up on their food in the dark. A shining light will bounce off a wolf spider's eyes. People can use flashlights to find wolf spiders in the dark. This is called "spider sniffing."

Digging a Hole

Most wolf spiders use burrows for homes. Some **species** make a trap door. This helps the spider hide. Other wolf spiders build a **turret** outside the entrance to their burrow. This helps keep water out.

Many wolf spider burrows are narrow. Only a few spots are wide enough for the spider to turn around.

Leg It Out

Wolf spiders use their legs for more than just running. Their legs are covered in tiny hairs. These hairs keep wolf spiders from sinking in water. They let wolf spiders run on top of water.

Wolf spider legs also keep them safe. If a **predator** catches a wolf spider by the leg, the spider can drop it off and escape. Over time, the spider will grow a new leg.

Map

Where They Live

Wolf spiders are known for their ability to live in many different places. Some are found in damp jungles. Others live in dry deserts. There are even wolf spiders in the Arctic.

Wolf Spiders around the World

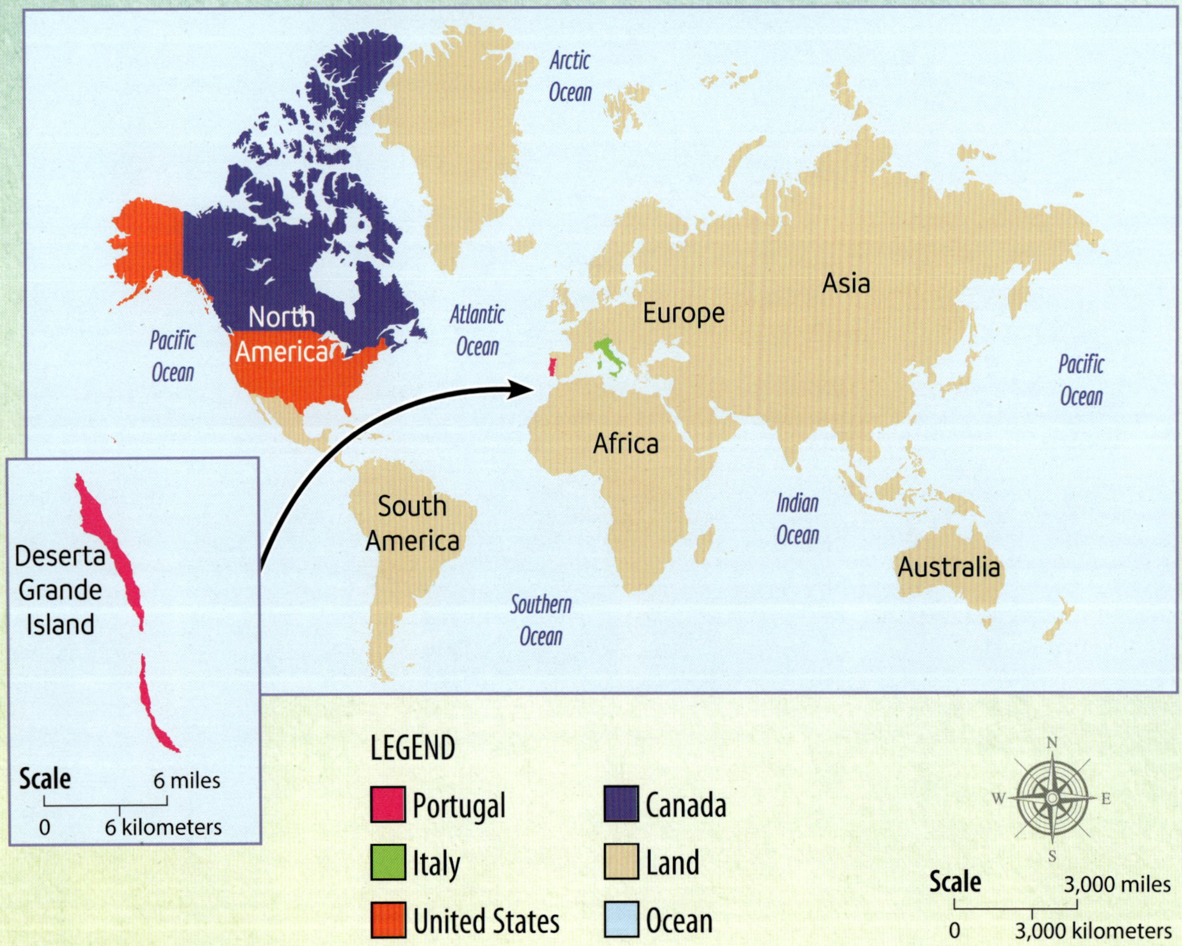

Arctic Wolf Spider

Arctic wolf spiders hunt small insects on the **tundra** of Canada and Alaska. Scientists believe there are about 4,000 of these spiders in every 2.5 acres (1 hectare) of the tundra.

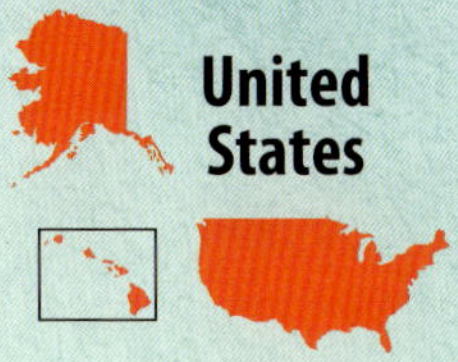

Carolina Wolf Spider

The Carolina wolf spider is the largest wolf spider in North America. It is the official state spider of South Carolina. Carolina wolf spiders live all over the United States and southern Canada.

Tarantula Wolf Spider

The tarantula wolf spider is named after the Italian city of Taranto. It was the first spider to be called a tarantula. However, it is actually a wolf spider. It was once believed that this spider's **venom** could be cured by dancing.

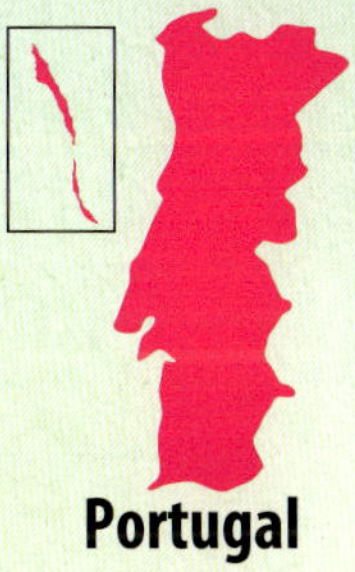

Deserta Grande Wolf Spider

The Deserta Grande wolf spider is only found on Deserta Grande Island. This small island is part of Portugal. The Deserta Grande wolf spider is **critically endangered**. Only about 4,000 are left on Earth.

Wolf Spider Safety

Wolf spiders can be very helpful. They eat many kinds of **pests**. These include grasshoppers and **aphids**.

Wolf spiders will bite people to protect themselves. A wolf spider's venom is painful. However, it is not usually dangerous. Some people are allergic to wolf spider venom. The spider's bite can harm them.

It is not a good idea to pick up a wolf spider. Instead, use a container or ask an adult to safely move it.

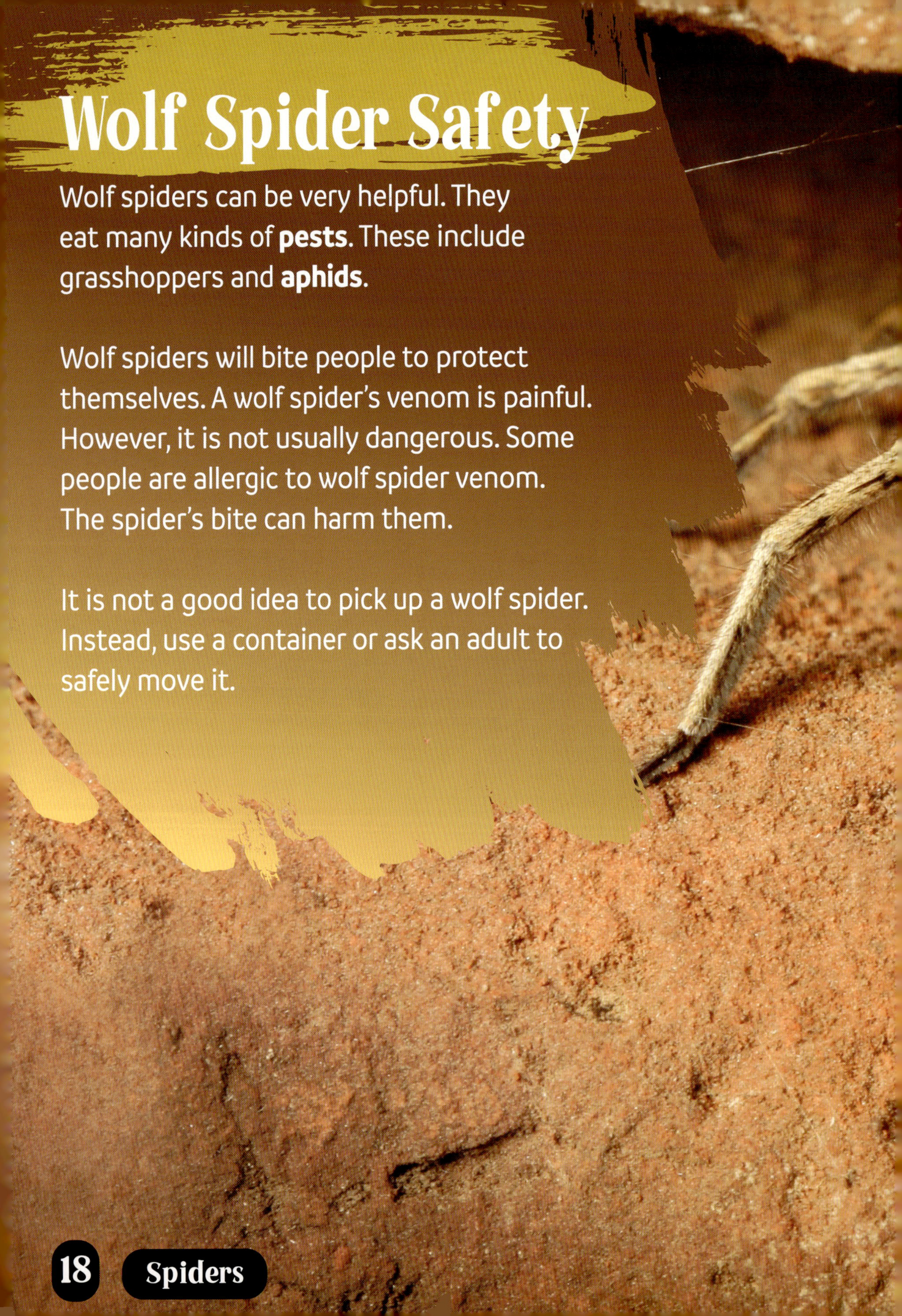

Activity

Create a Spider

There are many different kinds of spiders in the world. They all have certain features in common. However, each spider also has its own features. They help the spider live in its home.

Make your own spider by answering the following questions:

1. What is your spider called?
2. Where does it live?
3. What features does it share with other spiders?
4. What features help it live in its home? How do these features do this?
5. What does your spider look like?
6. Use pencils, markers, or crayons to draw your spider living in its home. Make sure to include all of its features.

Quiz

Test Your Knowledge

1
Do wolf spiders use webs to catch prey?

2
How many rows of eyes do wolf spiders have?

3
Where does a mother wolf spider carry her spiderlings?

4
Do wolf spiders see well at night?

5
What tool can be used to "spider sniff"?

6
What do some wolf spiders use to keep water out of their burrows?

7
What is the official spider of South Carolina?

8
Which wolf spiders live in the tundra?

ANSWERS 1. No 2. Three 3. On her back 4. Yes 5. A flashlight 6. Turrets 7. Carolina wolf spider 8. Arctic wolf spiders

Key Words

aphids: small insects that eat and destroy plants

burrows: underground homes dug by animals

camouflaged: something hidden by matching its surroundings

critically endangered: a plant or animal that is very rare and may soon disappear from Earth

mate: one member of a pair of animals that can reproduce, or have children

pedipalps: spider mouthparts that are used to feel and hold things

pests: animals that harm or bother humans

predator: an animal that hunts or kills other animals

prey: animals that are eaten by other animals

reflect: to bounce back

species: a group of related animals or organisms

spiderlings: baby spiders

tundra: treeless, frozen areas of land

turret: a tower or tower-shaped object

venom: a toxic substance produced by certain animals

Index

Get the best of both worlds.

AV2 bridges the gap between print and digital.

The expandable resources toolbar enables quick access to content including **videos**, **audio**, **activities**, **weblinks**, **slideshows**, **quizzes**, and **key words**.

Animated videos make static images come alive.

Resource icons on each page help readers to further **explore key concepts**.

Published by AV2
14 Penn Plaza, 9th Floor New York, NY 10122
Website: www.av2books.com

Library of Congress Control Number: 2019957560

ISBN 978-1-7911-2304-8 (hardcover)
ISBN 978-1-7911-2305-5 (softcover)
ISBN 978-1-7911-2306-2 (multi-user eBook)
ISBN 978-1-7911-2307-9 (single-user eBook)

Printed in Guangzhou, China
1 2 3 4 5 6 7 8 9 0 24 23 22 21 20

052020
101119

Designer: Terry Paulhus Project Coordinator: John Willis

Every reasonable effort has been made to trace ownership and to obtain permission to reprint copyright material. The publisher would be pleased to have any errors or omissions brought to its attention so that they may be corrected in subsequent printings.

The publisher acknowledges Alamy, Getty Images, iStock, Minden Pictures, and Shutterstock as its primary image suppliers for this title.
Page 17 top image © Oskar Liset Pryds Hansen https://www.inaturalist.org/photos/5917626